# California First-Year Law Students' Examination

# Essay Questions and Selected Answers

# October 2015

The State Bar of California
Committee of Bar Examiners / Office of Admissions

180 Howard Street • San Francisco, CA 94105-1639 • (415) 538-2300
845 South Figueroa Street • Los Angeles, CA 90017-2515 • (213) 765-1500

## ESSAY QUESTIONS AND SELECTED ANSWERS

## OCTOBER 2015

## CALIFORNIA FIRST-YEAR LAW STUDENTS' EXAMINATION

This publication contains the four essay questions from the October 2015 California First-Year Law Students' Examination and two selected answers for each question.

The answers were assigned high grades and were written by applicants who passed the examination. The answers were produced as submitted by the applicant, except that minor corrections in spelling and punctuation were made for ease in reading. They are reproduced here with the consent of the authors.

| Question Number | Subject |
| --- | --- |
| 1. | Contracts |
| 2. | Criminal Law |
| 3. | Torts |
| 4. | Contracts |

# October 2015

## ESSAY QUESTIONS

# California First-Year Law Students' Examination

## Answer all 4 questions.

Your answer should demonstrate your ability to analyze the facts in the question, to tell the difference between material facts and immaterial facts, and to discern the points of law and fact upon which the case turns. Your answer should show that you know and understand the pertinent principles and theories of law, their qualifications and limitations, and their relationships to each other.

Your answer should evidence your ability to apply the law to the given facts and to reason in a logical, lawyer-like manner from the premises you adopt to a sound conclusion. Do not merely show that you remember legal principles. Instead, try to demonstrate your proficiency in using and applying them.

If your answer contains only a statement of your conclusions, you will receive little credit. State fully the reasons that support your conclusions, and discuss all points thoroughly.

Your answer should be complete, but you should not volunteer information or discuss legal doctrines that are not pertinent to the solution of the problem.

You should answer according to legal theories and principles of general application.

# QUESTION 1

Painter and Developer entered into a contract under the terms of which Painter was to paint the interior of Developer's new apartment building for a price of $40,000. The contract called for work to begin on June 1 and to be completed on July 1.

Painter was ready to start work on June 1, but Developer told Painter that because of problems with the drywall contractor, Painter could not start work until June 15. To avoid the possibility of losing her employees, who might quit if forced to take a two-week layoff, Painter took another job, which was not completed until June 20, at which time Painter started work on Developer's building.

On July 15, Painter informed Developer that she would not be able to complete the project until August 15. Developer told her he would lose substantial rental income if the project was not completed by August 1, when university students, his prime market, began moving in. He asked her to hire additional help, but she refused, saying the job would be finished on August 15 or not at all. In an attempt to get the job completed sooner, Developer fired Painter and looked for another painting contractor.

The best price Developer could get to have another painting contractor finish the job was $30,000. Before firing Painter, Developer had paid Painter one-half of the contract price. Because the painting was completed late, Developer lost $10,000 in rental income. This rental income would not have been lost if the painting had been completed by August 1.

At the time Painter was fired, she was out-of-pocket for $5,000 in materials. She expected a profit of $5,000 had she been allowed to complete the contract.

Developer has sued Painter for breach of contract. Painter cross-complained against Developer for breach of contract.

1. Who breached the contract? Discuss.

2. Assuming Painter breached the contract, what damages, if any, would Developer be entitled to? Discuss.

3. Assuming Developer breached the contract, what damages, if any, would Painter be entitled to? Discuss.

# QUESTION 1: SELECTED ANSWER A

**1) Who breached the contract? Discuss.**

**DEVELOPER V. PAINTER**

The rights and remedies of parties to a contract depend on there being a valid contract and the terms and performance thereof. A contract is a promise or set of promises for the breach of which the law provides a remedy and the performance of which the law recognizes as a duty. An enforceable contract consists of MUTUAL ASSENT (VALID OFFER AND ACCEPTANCE), CONSIDERATION and NO DEFENSES.

GOVERNING LAW

The sale of goods, those items moveable and tangible at the time of identification to the contract are governed by the UCC. All other contracts are governed by the common law.

Here, the agreement calls for painting services, which are not moveable at the time of contract and thus not goods. The agreement is for services, governed by the common law. Therefore, the common law governs.

CONTRACT FORMATION

Here, a contract exists because certain and definite terms have been agreed Including Parties (Painter, Developer), Price ($40k), Quantity (1 job), Subject (Painting), Performance Date (June 1-July1). There has impliedly been acceptance and the consideration of legally sufficient, bargained-for exchange that induces performance and is a detriment to the promisee of $40,000 has been identified. The STATUTE OF FRAUDS, a requirement of a written expression for certain contract types does not apply here as the provision of painting services is not one of the 5 types (Marriage, Over a Year, Land, Executory, Guarantor). Therefore, there is an impliedly valid contract.

## CONTRACT TERMS

Here, the contract specified that performance was to begin June 1 and complete by July 1. There was no EXPRESS TIME IS OF THE ESSENCE clause; however the specificity of the dates of performance implies that time is a MATERIAL TERM.

## CONTRACT PERFORMANCE

## JUNE 1 - WAIVER OF START?

Here, on June 1, Painter was ready to start but an IMPLIED CONDITION PRECEDENT that the drywall be completed first was not satisfied. Therefore, because an IMPLIED CONDITION PRECEDENT was not satisfied, Painter's start was waived. Further, Painter took additional work to be completed June 20.

## JULY 15 - ANTICIPATORY BREACH?

ANTICIPATORY BREACH is the unequivocal communication of a repudiation of a contract duty before that duty is due to be performed. The act allows the non-breaching party to treat as a BREACH and immediately take all legal remedies and seek to mitigate.

BREACH is a non-performance of a required contract duty. A MINOR BREACH is where the contract is substantially performed but not completely. A MATERIAL BREACH is where the non-breaching party is deprived of the substantial benefit of the bargain.

Here, there is an ANTICIPATORY BREACH because Painter tells Developer that "she would not be able to complete the project until August 15," which is a date after which performance was due. The BREACH is a MAJOR BREACH because although Painter had commenced performance, the parties had expressly made time a MATERIAL TERM and the substantial change from July 1 to Aug 15 of 6 weeks to finish (longer than the original period of work) would deprive DEVELOPER of the substantial benefit of the bargain. Developer also indicates that his clients are students who begin moving in by August 1. Therefore, Painter anticipatorily breached the contract with Developer and allowed Developer to declare a breach and seek legal remedies and to mitigate.

**2) Assuming Painter breached the contract, what damages, if any, would Developer be entitled to? Discuss.**

DAMAGES

Damages are compensation for contract harm and include MONETARY DAMAGES and EQUITABLE RELIEF.

MONETARY DAMAGES

Monetary damages include EXPECTATION DAMAGES, CONSEQUENTIAL and RELIANCE DAMAGES.

EXPECTATION DAMAGES

EXPECTATION DAMAGES give the non-breaching party the "benefit of the bargain". Where there is a BREACH, the non-breaching party is allowed to cure. The cure would be the difference between the market price and the contract price for the completion of the contract.

Here, Developer would be entitled to EXPECTATION DAMAGES equal to the difference between the market price to finish of $30,000 and the contract price of $40,000 less the amount already paid of $20,000 or $20,000.

CONSEQUENTIAL DAMAGES

Under Hadley-Baxendale, CONSEQUENTIAL DAMAGES that are foreseeable, contemplated at the time of contracting, certain and mitigated are awarded as compensation.

Here, at the time of contracting, it was not known to Painter that Developer intended to rent his apartment to students by Aug 1. Because it was not contemplated, such consequential damages even if foreseeable and certain (rental income is certain) would not be awarded.

RELIANCE DAMAGES

RELIANCE DAMAGES are amounts spent in reliance on the contract that would be awarded as if the contract had never happened.

Here, because Painter had spent $5,000 in materials for the job that had not been applied to the job, Painter would receive and Developer would owe $5,000 in reliance damages. Therefore, Developer would owe Painter $5,000 in reliance damages.

Therefore, if PAINTER BREACHED, Developer would receive a net $15,000 from Painter for completion of the job.

EQUITABLE RELIEF

Based on QUANTUM MERUIT, if there is inequity as a result of an award, EQUITABLE RELIEF may be sought to better value the damages.

Here, if Painter's work was largely complete, QUANTUM MERUIT might suggest that EQUITABLE RELIEF be used to adjust the damages to reflect the value of the work completed by Painter prior to the breach.

**3) Assuming Developer breached the contract, what damages, if any, would Painter be entitled to? Discuss.**

DAMAGES. Supra.

EXPECTATION DAMAGES. Supra.

Here, if Developer has breached, Painter would be entitled to the "benefit of the bargain" or the $5,000 in expected profits. Therefore, Painter would be entitled to $5,000 in expectation damages.

CONSEQUENTIAL DAMAGES. Supra.

Here, if Developer has breached, Painter would be required to pay any consequential damages because Developer was the breaching party.

RELIANCE DAMAGES. Supra.

Here, if Developer has breached, Painter would still be entitled to the $5,000 in materials for the job in addition. Therefore, Painter would receive $5,000 in reliance damages.

Therefore, if DEVELOPER BREACHED, Painter would receive a net $10,000 from Developer for leaving the job.

# QUESTION 1:  SELECTED ANSWER B

**Question 1:**

## 1. Who Breached the Contract? Discuss.

**Applicable Law?**

The common law applies to contracts for the provision of services.  Here, the subject matter of the contract is the painting of an apartment building.  Painting is a service, something that requires labor as opposed to a sale of goods.   Therefore, the common law applies to this contract.

**Valid contract?**

Here the facts state that there was a contract between Painter and Developer; thus there are no issues of offer, acceptance, or consideration (Painting work by Painter, $40,000 payment to Painter by Developer).

**Defenses to Formation**

**Definiteness of Terms?**

Under the common law, a contract requires that quantity, time of performance, identity of parties, price and subject matter be identified in the contract.  The facts state the quantity - 1 apartment building to be painted, time - painting to take place between June 1 and July 1, parties - Painter and Developer, price - $40,000, and subject matter - painting of the apartment building have been identified.  Thus, the contract will not fail due to indefiniteness.

## Statute of Frauds:

The statute of frauds requires that certain contracts be written in order to be enforceable, including sale of goods contracts over $500, service contracts that cannot be completed within 1 year, promises for marriage, promises to answer for debt of another, and contracts for the sale of an interest in land.

The facts do not state whether the contract was made in writing. Here, none of these items apply to this contract. The contract performance time is just 1 month (June 1 to July 1), and although the contract involves painting work on a building, which is real estate, painting is a service, not a transfer of any title interest; therefore, the statute of frauds will not prevent enforcement of this contract.

## Implied Covenants of contract:

An implied covenant is an implied promise by one party to a contract to do something. Developer, in making the contract, made an implied covenant that the building drywall would be ready for painting by June 1.

## Conditions of contract:

A condition to performance is some event or action that must occur in order for the party to be charged to be found in breach.

Here, in order for the painting of the building to commence, there is an implied condition that the drywall must be completed, as drywall is a lower layer on a wall, and the paint is applied to the top of the drywall.

**Performance:**

The contract stated that the painting was to commence on June 1, and Painter was ready to start painting on June 1; however, Developer was not ready for the building to be painted, thus, Painter was unable to begin painting on June 1.

**Breach:**

A breach of contract is a failure of one party to a contract to perform his/her duties under the contract.

Painter will argue that Developer breached the contract on June 1 through an unequivocal statement that the building would not be ready for painting (drywall not ready) until June 15.

**Materiality of Breach**

A material breach is one that substantially negatively impacts the non-breaching party.

Developer's failure to have the building drywalled by June 1 as agreed to was a material breach, as this could cause a substantial loss of staff, who would have to take a two week layoff; had Painter known prior to contract formation that Developer wasn't going to be ready for painting until June 15, Painter likely would have attempted to find other work for his staff prior to Developer's breach.

**Excuse of Condition**

Developer's breach of his covenant (supra) to have the drywall prepared by June 1 was an excuse of the Painter's conditional performance to paint the building, because absent the drywall completion, the painting could not commence because paint must be applied to the drywall, not to the studs in the walls.

**Course of Performance:**

Course of performance refers to actions conducted by either party to the contract which will demonstrate what the parties actually agreed to. While Developer breached the condition of having drywall ready in time, Painter did not treat this breach as a full repudiation of the contract, but rather commenced work on the painting work on June 15.

Developer will argue that despite the delay in commencement of painting caused by Developer, Painter anticipatorily repudiated the contract by stating that the work would not be done until August 15. The difference in the originally agreed to start date (June 1) and completion date (July 1), was just one month, which would imply an agreed to completion time of one month from the start of painting. Painter completed his other project on June 20, which is approximately 55 days before his new estimated completion date of August 15. 55 days is much more than 1 month; therefore, Developer will argue that through the course of performance that altered the start date and by Painter stating unequivocally that he could not get done until August 15, it was Painter who breached.

Despite Developer's arguments, Developer was the breaching party.

## 2. Assuming Painter breached the contract, what damages, if any, would Developer be entitled to?

**Consequential Damages**

Consequential damages are awarded to compensate the non-breaching party for losses sustained as a consequence of the breach. As a consequence to the delay in the completion of the painting, Developer would not be able to rent the units in the building at their normal time, and lost $10,000 in income. Thus, $10,000 in consequential damages may be awarded.

**Expectation Damages**

Expectation damages are awarded to place the non-breaching party in the condition they would have been in had the contract not been breached.

In reliance on the contract, Developer had paid $15,000 to Painter. In addition, he ultimately had to pay another painter $30,000 to finish the job; thus his total cost of the contract was $45,000, which is $5,000 more than Developer had agreed to pay Painter. Because Developer would not have had to pay the additional $5,000 had Painter fully performed, Developer may be awarded $5,000 in expectation damages. This would put him back in the position of having only paid a net of ($45,000 minus $5,000 damages) $40,000 in exchange for a painted building.

**Duty to Mitigate Damages**

When a party to a contract breaches, the non-breaching party has a duty to mitigate damages. Here, Developer fulfilled this duty by soliciting bids and locating another painter to complete the painting job.

**3. Assuming Developer breached the contract, what damages, if any, would Painter be entitled to? Discuss**

**Expectation damages**

Rule: Supra

The facts state that while the contract price was $40,000, Developer only paid Painter $15,000. This is a difference in $25,000. Had the contract been fully performed, Painter would have received the additional $25,000; thus $25,000 in expectation damages may be awarded

**Duty to mitigate damages**

Rule supra

Upon hearing that the drywall would not be ready in time for painting, Painter went out and found another painting job for her and her staff to complete; thus by finding other work which would generate income during the waiting period, Painter fulfilled the duty as a nonbreaching party to mitigate damages.

# QUESTION 2

Bob was an underpaid teller at Bank. On his lunch hour one day, he went into a store where he noticed a valuable necklace on the counter. He picked it up and put it in his pocket. Clare, a clerk at the store, approached Bob and asked him to put the necklace back. Bob punched Clare, returned the necklace to the counter, and fled back to Bank where he began waiting on customers.

One customer was Fred, Bob's close friend, who put down a ten-dollar bill and asked Bob for a roll of quarters. Bob then told Fred that he would secretly pass him one hundred dollars if Fred would later give him one-half. Fred agreed and later the two split the cash.

The next morning when Bob went to work, Marilyn, the bank manager, began questioning him in her office. Alarmed at this, Bob grabbed a letter opener and stabbed Marilyn in her arm. Then Bob fled outside, jumped in a car, and drove to the house of Gina, his girlfriend. He told Gina what had happened. Gina decided to call the police, but Bob knocked her unconscious, put her in his car and went to Fred's house to hide her.

Finding the door to Fred's house locked, Bob broke in the door and hid Gina inside. At that point Fred appeared and protested to Bob. Bob struck Fred, pushing him down. As Fred fell, he knocked over a lamp and started a fire. Bob panicked and ran out of the house. The house began to burn. Fred got out alive, but Gina died in the fire.

What crimes, if any, did Bob commit? Discuss.

# QUESTION 2: SELECTED ANSWER A

## STATE V. BOB

## LARCENY

The trespassory taking and carrying away of the property of another with the specific intent to permanently deprive owner thereof.

Bob picked up a valuable necklace that was on the counter at the bank. The taking was trespassory because it did not belong to Bob and he did not have permission to take it. He put it in his pocket; this is sufficient movement to constitute as a carrying away. The property did not belong to Bob, so it was that of another's. Bob will argue that he did not intend to keep it, especially since he put the necklace back. The State will argue that since the facts indicate that Bob was an "underpaid teller" it is likely that Bob specifically meant to take it and deprive the owner thereof so he could have the value. Additionally, only after he was caught did he put it back.

*Bob is guilty of larceny.*

## ASSAULT

Assault is either the substantial step towards the perpetration of an intended battery or the intentional placing of another in reasonable apprehension of an imminent harmful application of force.

### Substantial Step

Bob raised his arm to swing to punch Clare. The raising and swinging of his arm is a substantial step towards the perpetration of the subsequent hitting.

*Bob is guilty of this type of assault, but it will merge with the subsequent battery.*

### Reasonable Apprehension

Since Clare was facing Bob, she would have been able to see him raise his arm to swing at her. Given that she had just caught him stealing a necklace, Clare could have anticipated a violent response and would have been in reasonable apprehension when she saw him raise his arm.

*Bob is guilty of this type of assault.*

## BATTERY

The unlawful application of force to another's person

Bob punched Clare. Punching is an application of force and it was applied to Clare, another person. Bob did not have a right to do so; thus it was unlawful.

*Bob is guilty of battery.*

## SOLICITATION TO COMMIT EMBEZZLEMENT

Solicitation is the counseling, enticing or inciting of another with the intent for that person to commit a crime. Embezzlement is the fraudulent conversion of rightfully entrusted property with the intent to permanently deprive the owner thereof.

When Fred gave Bob a roll of quarters and asked for a ten-dollar bill, Bob told Fred that he would secretly give him $100. Bob enticed Fred to take the $100, instead of the $10 that he was owed, therefore depriving the bank (the owner) of the additional $90. Since Bob was a bank teller, he was rightfully entrusted with the money that he gave to Fred, but he converted the remaining $90 for purposes that were inconsistent with the Bank's ownership.

## CONSPIRACY TO COMMIT EMBEZZLEMENT

An agreement between two or more parties to commit a crime.

Embezzlement is the fraudulent conversion of rightfully entrusted property with the intent to permanently deprive the owner thereof.

Bob asked Fred to take the $100 and to split the extra cash with him. Fred agreed. Bob handed Fred the cash, which was a step towards the completion of the embezzlement.

*Bob is guilty of conspiracy with Fred.*

## EMBEZZLEMENT OF $100

Embezzlement is the fraudulent conversion of rightfully entrusted property with the intent to permanently deprive the owner thereof.

When Fred gave Bob a roll of quarters and asked for a ten-dollar bill, Bob told Fred that he would secretly give him $100. Bob enticed Fred to take the $100, instead of the $10 that he was owed, therefore depriving the bank (the owner) of the additional $90. Since Bob was a bank teller, he was rightfully entrusted with the money that he gave to Fred, but he converted the remaining $90 for purposes that were inconsistent with the Bank's ownership. Bob may argue that he was merely in custody, rather than in possession, of the cash. If the court finds that this is true, then he will be guilty of larceny instead of embezzlement. See discussion infra.

*Bob is guilty of embezzlement.*

## LARCENY OF $100

The trespassory taking and carrying away of the property of another with the specific intent to permanently deprive owner thereof.

Fred gave Bob a roll of quarters and asked for a ten-dollar bill. Bob told Fred that he would secretly give him $100. Bob enticed Fred to take the $100, instead of the $10 that he was owed, therefore depriving the bank (the owner) of the additional $90. If the court decides that Bob is a low-level employee, they will find that he only had custody over the cash instead of possession and will be found guilty for larceny instead of embezzlement.

## AGGRAVATED ASSAULT OF MARILYN

Assault is either the substantial step towards the perpetration of an intended battery or the intentional placing of another in reasonable apprehension of an imminent harmful application of force.

### Substantial Step

Bob grabbed a letter opener to stab Marilyn. The grabbing and moving of his arm is a substantial step towards the perpetration of the subsequent stabbing.

*Bob is guilty of this type of assault, but it will merge with the subsequent battery.*

### Reasonable Apprehension

Since Marilyn was facing Bob, she would have been able to see him grab the letter opener. Given that she had just caught him stealing, Marilyn could have anticipated a violent response and would have been in reasonable apprehension when she saw him raise his arm with the opener.

### Aggravation

The letter opener was used as a deadly weapon, thus making this an aggravated crime.

*Bob is guilty of this type of aggravated assault.*

## AGGRAVATED BATTERY

The unlawful application of force to another's person

Bob stabbed Marilyn. Stabbing is an application of force and it was applied to Marilyn, another person. Bob did not have a right to do so; thus it was unlawful.

## Aggravation

The letter opener was used as a deadly weapon, thus making this an aggravated crime.

*Bob is guilty of aggravated battery.*

## ASSAULT of Gina

Assault is either the substantial step towards the perpetration of an intended battery or the intentional placing of another in reasonable apprehension of an imminent harmful application of force.

## Substantial Step

Bob raised his arm to swing to punch Gina. The raising and swinging of his arm is a substantial step towards the perpetration of the subsequent hitting.

*Bob is guilty of this type of assault, but it will merge with the subsequent battery.*

## Reasonable Apprehension

Since Gina was facing Bob, she would have been able to see him raise his arm to swing at her. Given that she had just threatened to call the police, Gina could have anticipated a violent response and would have been in reasonable apprehension when she saw him raise his arm.

*Bob is guilty of this type of assault.*

## BATTERY

The unlawful application of force to another's person

Bob knocked Gina out. Punching is an application of force and it was applied to Gina, another person. Bob did not have a right to do so; thus it was unlawful.

*Bob is guilty of battery.*

## KIDNAPPING

The unlawful confinement and asportation of another.

Bob knocked Gina out and made her unconscious.  Since Gina was unconscious and could not escape, she was confined. Bob then put her in the car and took her to Fred's house.  This is movement and asportation of Gina.

*Bob is guilty of kidnapping*

## AGGRAVATED BURGLARY

### Common Law
Burglary is the breaking and entering into the dwelling of another in the nighttime with the specific intent to commit a felony therein.

### Breaking and entering
Bob went to Fred's house.  Since the door was locked, he broke it.  This is sufficient for a breaking.  Bob then entered.

### Dwelling of another
Facts indicate that this was Fred's house. A dwelling

### Nighttime
The facts do not indicate whether this event happens at night or not.  Night is defined as the period between sunset and sunrise.  Since the fact pattern began in the morning, it is likely still the daytime.

### Specific Intent to Commit a Felony
Bob intended to hide unconscious Gina in Fred's house.  As discussed supra, this is a kidnapping and a felony sufficient enough for this element.

*Since it is likely not the nighttime, Bob is not guilty of common law burglary. However, if it is the nighttime, then he would be guilty.*

## MODERN LAW BURGLARY

The trespassory entering into any structure with the intent to commit a crime therein.

### Trespassory

Bob did not have permission to be in Fred's house. Thus his entry was trespassory.

### Any Structure

Fred's house is a structure.

### Intent to commit a crime

Bob intended to commit kidnapping as discussed supra.

## AGGRAVATION

Since the house was occupied by Fred when Bob broke in, this crime is aggravated.

*Bob is guilty of aggravated burglary.*

## AGGRAVATED ARSON

### Common Law

The malicious burning of the dwelling house of another.

Bob pushed Fred, causing him to knock over a lamp and start a fire. Bob will argue that he did not intend for the house to catch fire, and therefore his action was not malicious. The State will argue that he should have reasonably expected and known that pushing Fred would have caused the fire. Since the facts indicate the house began to burn, it is likely that at least charring to the structure had occurred.

*If the court finds that Bob should have known pushing Bob would cause fire, then he will be guilty of common law arson. If court finds he did not know, then he will not be found to be malicious and will not be guilty.*

## Modern Law

The malicious burning of any structure.

Fred's house is a structure. See discussion supra.

## AGGRAVATION

Since the house was occupied by Fred when the fire started, this crime would be aggravated.

## HOMICIDE OF GINA

Homicide is the killing of a human being by another human being.

Bob pushed Fred, causing a fire which killed Gina.

## Actual Cause

But for Bob pushing Fred and causing a fire, Gina would not have died when and how she did.

## Proximate Cause

Bob will argue that it is not foreseeable that pushing Fred into a lamp would have caused a fire. State will argue that pushing a person into a lamp, which is either electrical or open fire, it is reasonably foreseeable that a fire could catch on the house and cause death to people within the house.

*Bob is the actual and proximate cause to Gina's death.*

## MURDER

*The unlawful killing of another human with malice aforethought. Malice may be proven in one of four ways:*

### Specific Intent to Kill

Bob pushed Fred into a lamp, causing the lamp to catch the house on fire, killing Gina. Bob will argue that in pushing Fred, he did not specifically intend to kill Gina; he intended to harm Fred.

*State will not be able to prove malice under this theory.*

### Intent to Cause Serious Bodily Harm

Bob pushed Fred into a lamp, causing the lamp to catch the house on fire, killing Gina. Bob will argue that in pushing Fred, he did not specifically intend to harm Gina; he intended to harm Fred.

*State will not be able to prove malice under this theory.*

### Depraved Heart Act

State will argue that pushing Fred into a lamp, while Gina was unconscious in the house was a wanton and reckless disregard for the value of human life. State will argue that Bob should have reasonably foreseen the risk of fire and acted recklessly in pushing Fred, knowing that Gina could not escape in the case of a fire.

State will likely be able to prove malice under this theory.

### Felony Murder Rule

Gina's death occurred during the perpetration of a burglary. Bob may argue that the burglary was complete as he had already broken into the house and Gina was kidnapped. However, State will argue that the burglary had not been completed because Bob had not reached a place of safety. In fact, he was fighting with Fred in attempts to get away.

*State will likely be able to prove malice under this theory.*

## FIRST-DEGREE MURDER

*First-degree murder is murder that is committed with the intent to kill with premeditation and deliberation, through bomb, poison, ambush, torture or mutilation, or through the commission of an inherently dangerous felony.*

Bob will argue that he did not have the intent to kill, and thus could not have premeditated or deliberated. However, State will argue that Gina's death occurred during the perpetration of a burglary. Bob may argue that the burglary was complete as he had already broken into the house and Gina was kidnapped. However, State will argue that the burglary had not been completed because Bob had not reached a place of safety. In fact, he was fighting with Fred in attempts to get away. Bob may also argue that burglary and kidnapping are not inherently dangerous felonies.

*Bob is likely guilty of first-degree murder under the felony murder rule.*

## SECOND-DEGREE MURDER

Second-degree murder is murder that is committed with the specific intent to kill, without premeditation, with the specific intent to cause serious bodily harm, depraved heart act, or a felony insufficient to support felony murder rule.

If the State is unable to prove first-degree murder under the felony murder rule, then they may argue the depraved heart act and that pushing Fred into a lamp, while Gina was unconscious in the house, was a wanton and reckless disregard for the value of human life. State will argue that Bob should have reasonably foreseen the risk of fire and acted recklessly in pushing Fred, knowing that Gina could not escape in the case of a fire.

*At the very least, Bob will be guilty of second-degree murder.*

# QUESTION 2: SELECTED ANSWER B

PEOPLE v. BOB

## Larceny of Necklace

Under common law, Larceny is the trespassory taking and carrying away of the property of another with the intent to permanently deprive.

Here, there was a "taking" when Bob put the necklace in his pocket from the store counter. There was a "carrying away" because he "moved" the necklace from its original location and he had the intent to permanently deprive because he put it in his pocket to steal a "valuable necklace" and when he got caught by the store clerk, he "returned the necklace to the counter and fled" back to his work.

Therefore, Bob will be charged with larceny of the necklace.

## Assault on Clare (store clerk)

Under criminal law, assault is the intentional act to cause a battery or immediate apprehension of a battery, the harmful or offensive touching of another person.

Here, when Clare approached Bob and told him to put the necklace back, Bob punched Clare. Bob "intentionally" acted to commit a battery on Clare and the charge of assault will be included with the higher charge of battery.

## Battery on Clare

Under criminal law, battery is the intentional harmful or offensive touching of another person.

Here, as discussed supra, when Bob "punched Clare" he intended to punch her and commit battery on her because she caught him stealing the necklace.

Therefore, Bob will be charged with battery on Clare.

## Solicitation of Fred (friend) for embezzlement

Under criminal law, Solicitation is the urging of another person to commit a crime. The crime of solicitation is completed once the urging occurs and it does not matter if the person urged actually completes the crime or not. The crime of solicitation merges with the urged crime, if completed, and the person is vicariously liable for those crimes under the theory of accomplice liability.

Here, when Bob told Fred that he would "secretly pass him a one hundred dollar bill" instead of the roll of quarters that he requested, Bob was soliciting, "urging" Fred to commit a crime of accepting stolen property that he was embezzling from the bank. Because the "urging" was completed, Bob will be charged with the solicitation of Fred for the crime of embezzlement.

## Conspiracy with Fred for Embezzlement

Under common law, Conspiracy is an agreement between 2 or more people to work toward an illegal goal. Modernly, an overt act is required in furtherance of the commission of the crime / conspiracy goal. The crime of conspiracy does not "merge" with other crimes so the defendant may be charged with both the crime of conspiracy as well as the completed crimes that are also committed.

Here, when Bob told Fred that he would secretly pass him the $100 and they would split it AND when Fred "agreed" and later split the cash with Bob, there was an "agreement" between Bob and Fred to steal / embezzle the $100 from the bank, an illegal goal.
Bob will be charged with a separate charge of conspiracy with Fred.

## Embezzlement of bank $100

Under criminal law, Embezzlement is the taking of money with the intent to permanently deprive or putting at substantial risk, money or items that are lawfully in your possession that legally belong to someone else.

Here, when Bob purposely gave Fred the $100 instead of the roll of quarters, he took the money that was "lawfully in his possession" because he was a bank teller and used the money to perform his job. When Bob gave the $100 to Fred for them "to split the money" he intended to permanently deprive the bank of this money and did not intend to return it.

Therefore, Bob will be charged with embezzlement.

## Assault of Marilyn (bank manager)

Assault is defined supra. Here, when Bob became alarmed when Marilyn began questioning him about the $100, he stabbed her in the arm with a letter opener. Because his "intent" was to cause her bodily harm and apprehension, Bob committed assault on Marilyn.

Bob will be charged with assault of Marilyn which will merge with the charge of Battery if he is successfully charged.

## Battery of Marilyn

Battery is defined supra. Here, when Bob intentionally "stabbed Marilyn in the arm with a letter opener", he committed a "harmful and offensive touching" to Marilyn.

Therefore, Bob will be charged with the battery of Marilyn.

## Larceny of Car

Larceny is defined supra. Here, when Bob fled outside the bank, because he "jumped in a car", it is presumed that it was not his car. If in fact, the car was not his or he did not have permission to use, a larceny may have been committed (grand theft) since he "took and carried" (drove away) the car of someone else. If Bob had the intent to NOT return the car, but to keep it or discard it when he was done with it, then there was an "intent to permanently deprive" and the elements of larceny are met.

If, however, Bob was just "borrowing" the car in his moment of panic to flee the bank because he had just stabbed Marilyn in the arm, then this element may not be met if he did not have the "intent to permanently deprive" the rightful owner. Additionally, it must also be considered that Bob's fleeing may be considered part of the chain of events from the stabbing of Marilyn since he had not yet reached a place of relative safety.

Therefore, Bob may be charged with larceny of the car.

## Kidnapping of Gina (girlfriend)

Under criminal law, kidnapping is the wrongful taking or confinement of another person against their will. Under common law, it was required that the victim be transported across state lines. However, modernly that requirement has been dropped and is no longer required.

Here, because Bob knocked Gina unconscious and took her and put her in his car against her will because she was going to call the police, Bob "wrongfully took" Gina and "confined" her to the car when she was unconscious.

Therefore, Bob will be charged with the kidnapping of Gina.

## Assault / Battery of Gina

Assault and battery are discussed supra. Here, when Bob knocked Gina unconscious, he committed assault and battery on her. He will also be charged with battery in addition to kidnapping Gina.

## Burglary of Fred's house

Under common law, burglary is the breaking and entering the dwelling house of another at nighttime with the intent to commit a felony inside. Modernly, the rule has been extended to include any structure at any time of day and includes larceny as the intended crime, even if it is not a felony by statute.

In this case, Bob went to Fred's house to hide Gina whom he had kidnapped. Because Fred's house was "locked", Bob "broke the door and hid Gina inside" without Fred's permission or knowledge. Therefore, Bob both under common law and modernly committed "breaking and entering". However, the facts do not indicate the time of day. If it was during daytime the common law element would not be met. However, modernly this requirement is waived. Because Bob entered "Fred's house" this is the dwelling house of another. Bob intended to break into Fred's house to "hide Gina who had kidnapped", which is a felony.

The defense may argue that Bob had already committed the kidnapping when he knocked Gina unconscious and put her in the car, so the requirement to commit a felony inside of Fred's house is not met because he had already committed that crime. However, the prosecution will argue that Bob was still in the commission of committing the crime of kidnapping which would last the entire duration of her illegal confinement including when he took her to Fred's house to "hide her".

Therefore, it is likely that Bob will be charged modernly with Burglary of Fred's house.

## Assault / Battery of Fred

Assault and battery are discussed supra. Here, when Bob struck Fred when he "protested to Bob", and Bob "pushed him down", Bob committed assault and battery of Fred.

## Arson of Fred's house

Under common law, Arson is the malicious burning of the dwelling of another. Modernly, the rule has been extended to include any structure and malice means "with wrongful intent". The burning must include more than smoke and must include damage to include charring and actual burning.

In this case, because Fred fell and knocked over the lamp and started the fire, Bob did not intend to commit arson as he did not want or intend to start a fire.

Bob will not be charged with the arson for the burning of Fred's house.

## Homicide / Murder of Gina in Fire

Homicide is the unlawful killing of another, which includes murder and manslaughter. Murder is the unlawful killing of another with malice aforethought. Malice aforethought can be accomplished in one of four ways: 1) intent to kill, 2) intent to cause severe bodily injury, 3) an extremely reckless disregard for an unjustifiably high risk to human life or 4) through the Felony Murder Rule.

FELONY MURDER RULE

The felony murder rule applies a first-degree murder charge to the defendant if the death occurred as a result of the commission of an independent inherently dangerous felony (burglary, arson, rape, robbery and / or kidnapping).

Here, as discussed supra, Bob may be charged with both burglary and kidnapping and therefore the death of Gina occurred during the commission of an inherently dangerous felony and therefore malice is presumed for a charge of first-degree murder.

Therefore, Bob will likely be charged with first-degree murder under the Felony Murder Doctrine for the death of Gina in the fire.

## FIRST-DEGREE MURDER

First-degree murder is murder that requires premeditation, deliberation and a specific intent to kill. Here the facts do not support that Bob intended the death of anyone and he did not plan in advance the death of Gina or anyone else.

Therefore, Bob will not be charged with first-degree murder because there was no premeditation or specific intent to kill.

## SECOND-DEGREE MURDER

All murder other than first-degree murder is second-degree murder, which requires a wanton or reckless disregard or an unjustifiable risk to human life. Here, it can be argued that Bob's actions were wanton and reckless in that "he panicked and ran out of the house as it began to burn".

However, although a strong case can be made for second-degree murder, Bob will be charged with first-degree murder under felony murder.

## AFFIRMATIVE DUTY TO ACT

A person generally does not have a duty to assist others unless the person created that person's peril. Here, because Bob knocked Gina unconscious, kidnapped her and took her to Fred's house which caught on fire, he had a duty to assist her in her peril and to attempt to save her.

Because Bob fled and did not attempt to assist Gina out of the burning fire when he had an affirmative duty because he placed her in peril, Bob will be charged with the murder of Gina.

VOLUNTARY MANSLAUGHTER

Under criminal law, voluntary manslaughter is the intentional killing of another person that would be murder but for the existence of legally adequate provocation.

Here, there is not evidence to support that a reasonable person would have been provoked to act as Bob did under the same circumstances.

Therefore, Bob does not have a mitigating defense of adequate provocation and voluntary manslaughter will not apply.

INVOLUNTARY MANSLAUGHTER

Under criminal law, involuntary manslaughter is the unintentional killing of another person by means of gross criminal negligence, a deliberate breach of a pre-existing duty to protect others from risk of harm OR by recklessness, a deliberate creation of risk to others.

Here, because Bob did not intend to kill Gina, but his acts were extremely reckless, Bob would at a minimum be charged with involuntary manslaughter if the felony murder charge did not hold up.

# QUESTION 3

David owns a herd of dairy animals from which he produces and sells milk and cheese. The animals in his herd are the product of cross-breeding domestic goats and a wild breed of sheep. They have the appearance and size of large goats, but have the much more aggressive character of bighorn sheep. In fact, the males have large curved horns similar to those of the bighorn and become aggressive when agitated.

One of the locks on a gate into a pen that held 40 of these animals was beginning to pull free from the wooden support post to which the lock was attached; a close inspection would have revealed that the wood was rotting around the screws that attached the lock to the 10-year-old post. Unfortunately, David failed to examine the gate support post when he performed his regular semi-annual inspection of the fencing on his land. Eventually the lock in fact pulled out, the gate swung open, and the animals wandered onto neighboring land.

Peter, David's next-door neighbor, found most of the animals on his land. Peter attempted to herd the animals back onto David's land, using an electric cattle prod to deliver shocks to them when they wouldn't move as he wished. When Peter shocked one of the larger horned males, it turned and rammed him, knocking him to the ground. After Peter was driven to the ground, the animal continued butting him, striking Peter quite a few times in the head and upper body. The attack left Peter with a serious concussion and broken bones.

Peter went to the local hospital emergency room (ER), where his broken bones were set. Even though Peter mentioned having a headache, the ER doctor and nurses didn't examine him for concussion or other head injury. Peter failed to report to them that the animal had directly struck his head. Later that day, Peter suffered a cerebral hemorrhage (bleeding in the brain), with paralysis in his upper limbs.

1. What tort causes of action, if any, can Peter reasonably assert against David? Discuss.

2. What defenses, if any, can David reasonably raise? Discuss.

3. What damages, if any, will Peter be able to obtain against David? Discuss.

# QUESTION 3: SELECTED ANSWER A

1. **Peter vs. David**

**Strict Liability**

Strict Liability for wild animals or domesticated animals with known dangerous propensities arises when damages or injuries are caused by either wild animals or domesticated animals. Strict liability is liability without fault. As long as plaintiff can show causation and damages resulting from actions of above referenced animals and the damages caused resulted from the nature which makes such animals dangerous, plaintiffs are entitled to recover.

Here, David owned a herd of dairy animals. Although goats are domestic animals, they were cross-bred with a wild breed of sheep. In addition, they have the aggressive character of bighorn sheep, which is known to the owner. Peter was driven to the ground by one of the larger horned males which escaped the farm. The animal rammed Peter, knocking him to the ground and butted him. Animal acted based on its nature and known dangerous propensities making David strictly liable for Peter's injuries. Peter sustained a concussion and broken bones, which are foreseeable outcomes of being rammed by a wild bighorn sheep.

David will be strictly liable for injuries sustained by Peter.

**Negligence**

In order to prevail in a negligence action, Plaintiff must show that defendant owed him/her a duty of care, said duty was breached, damages were sustained and said damages were caused by Defendant's breach.

## Duty

David owed a duty of care of a reasonably prudent person to avoid subjecting others to unreasonable risk of harm. Owning cross-bred animals, the standard of care would be to exercise care to ensure securing the animals. This would include inspection and maintenance of the lock of the gate and fences. Although he conducted semi-annual inspection of the fencing of his land, he failed to examine the gate support. David owed a duty to all foreseeable plaintiffs. Under **Palsgraf** case, the majority Cardozo view imposed duty on all plaintiffs within the zone of danger. Peter was a next-door neighbor and was therefore within the zone of danger under Cardozo view. Under Andrews view, which was the minority view, the duty of care is owed to everyone.

David owed a duty of care to Peter.

## Breach of Duty

Breach occurs when defendant's act falls below the standard of care established. Here, the standard of care was that of a reasonably prudent farmer, one that would exercise care to keep his animals within his farm. His duty included securing the lock of the gate which, as facts stipulate, David failed to do.

David breached his duty to Peter by failure to examine the gate.

## Actual cause- "But-for"

David's breach was the actual cause of Peter's injuries since but for David's failure to examine the gate and secure it, keeping the animals within the farm, Peter would not be injured by the bighorn sheep. David was also a substantial factor for Peter's injuries sustained by ER doctor's failure to examine for concussion.

Therefore, David was the actual cause of Peter's injuries.

<u>Proximate Cause</u>

David's failure to examine the gate was the proximate cause of Peter's injuries. Proximate cause has to pass the foreseeability test. It was foreseeable that had the gate lock failed to be secured or properly supported, the animals would escape and injure someone. David was also the proximate cause of injuries sustained by ER doctor's failure to examine as it was a natural and foreseeable consequence, since he created the peril. Although the ER's failure to examine was an intervening cause, it was foreseeable and both tortfeasors contributed to Peter's injuries.

David was the proximate cause of Peter's injuries.

<u>Damages</u>

Peter sustained head injury, concussion and broken bones. He will recover both for pain and suffering and for medical bills incurred.

**Trespass to Land**

Interference and physical intrusion upon another's land without consent.

Here, David's sheep entered Peter's land without permission. He was in charge of them.

Peter will be able to recover for damages to his land.

**Joint Tortfeasors.**

Both David and hospital staff contributed to final damages sustained by Peter. They were substantial factors causing Peter's damages. Since they are jointly and severally liable, Peter can recover from both or either the full amount of damages and the tortfeasors may sue each other for contribution or indemnification.

## 2.    David's Defenses

### Assumption of Risk

Assumption of risk defense can be raised when Plaintiff knew and appreciated the risk of harm involved and exposed himself/herself to said risk.

Here, David may argue that Peter assumed risk of getting injured and rammed by animals, when he attempted to herd the animals back onto David's land. He used an electric cattle prod which provoked and aggravated sheep. However, this defense will fail because Peter was not aware of the cross-breeding and did not know the sheep had dangerous propensities.

### Contributory Negligence

Under tort law, contributory negligence defense may be raised when Plaintiff's own actions contribute to his/her injuries. In some jurisdictions, it can be a complete bar to recovery.

Here, David may assert that Peter contributed to his own injuries by provoking animals with an electric prod and further contributed to his cerebral hemorrhage and paralysis by failure to report to ER doctors and hospital of head injury. However, this defense will fail because Peter was not a doctor and being under hospital care, he was expected to be examined properly. As for provoking, he acted as a reasonable person would in Peter's position in attempting to herd animals back to David.

This defense will fail.

**Comparative Negligence**

Under comparative negligence, if Peter is found to have contributed to his own injuries, the damages will be apportioned based on fault.

David will argue that by provoking animals and failure to report to hospital of head injury, Peter contributed to his own injuries. This defense will fail, however, even if a small percentage of fault is placed on Peter, his damages will be reduced by said amount.

### 3. Peter's Damages against David

**Special Damages**

Special damages include medical bills, loss of earnings, loss of earning capacity.

Peter incurred hospital bills and due to his paralysis has likely lost earning capacity.

Peter will be able to recover said damages.

**General Damages**

Pain and suffering, loss of enjoyment can be recovered.

Peter sustained pain and suffering when sheep rammed and for further injuries sustained at the hospital.

He will be able to recover for general damages which will also include loss of ability to enjoy ordinary daily living activities due to his paralysis.

# QUESTION 3: SELECTED ANSWER B

**TORT LAW/QUESTION #3**

**What tort causes of action if any can Peter reasonably assert against David? Discuss.**

**Peter v. David**

**Strict Liability**

Under strict liability theory, **liability is imposed without fault.**

Strict liability attaches to cause of action from possession of domestic and wild animals, or ultrahazardous/abnormally dangerous activities on one's land.

Here, strict liability will attach to an owner, David, who has a herd of dairy animals which the owner uses to produce and sell milk for commercial purposes.

The owner or possessor of trespassing animals is strictly liable for any damage caused to person or property. The damage must result from **the dangerous propensity of the animal(s)**, that make the animals wild or dangerous in the first place.

**Trespassing animals**

The owner or possessor of a herd of domestic animals is strictly liable in tort for trespass for any damage caused by such animal, to property and person.

David will be liable for any damage caused by his trespassing animals.

## Wild Animals

Here, David owns a breed of herd of cross-breeding domestic goats and a wild breed of sheep. They have the appearance and size of large goats, but have the much more **aggressive character of bighorn sheep.** In fact, according to the facts of the case, the males have large curved horns similar to those of the bighorn and become aggressive when agitated.

David as an owner or breeder will know the dangerous propensity of these animals and will be strictly liable for any damage from their dangerous propensity.

Here, the facts indicate these were cross-bred animals with dangerous propensity, namely that of a bighorn sheep with large curved horns who become aggressive when agitated.

Peter, David's next-door neighbor, found most of the animals on his land and attempted to herd the animals back to David's land. One of the animals became agitated when prodded with an electric cattle prod and turned and rammed Peter, knocking him to the ground. Afterwards, the animal continued to butt him, striking Peter quite a few times in the head and upper body. Peter was left with a serious concussion and broken bones.

David will argue that he behaved reasonably under the circumstances, but regardless, given the natural propensity of this particular breed, David is strictly liable for injuries he suffered by the animals butting him with large curved horns.

David may argue assumption of risk by Peter, but he is likely to be held liable for his animals goring him to his injury.

David is likely to be strictly liable for David's physical and property injury by his animals.

## Negligence

Peter may have a cause of action for Negligence, if Peter can establish that David owed him a duty, and David breached that duty, and the breach of which inflicted injury, both actually and proximately caused by his breach, resulting in physical injury.

## Duty

Duty is created when a defendant does an act which foreseeably causes an unreasonable risk of harm to others. The question arises whether the defendant exercised reasonable care once that duty arose.

## Standard of Care/General duty

The standard of care used to determine general duty of care is one exercised by a reasonable person of ordinary prudence under the same or similar circumstances.

Here, David owed a duty of due care to keep his herd of cross-bred and potentially dangerous animals in a safe place and manner.

One of the locks on a gate into the pen that held 40 of his animals was beginning to pull free from the wooden support post to which the lock was attached. Notably, a close inspection would have revealed that the wood was rotting around the screws that attached the lock the 10-year-old post.. Unfortunately, David failed to examine the gate support post when he performed his regular semi-annual inspection of the fencing on his land.

Thus, David owned a duty of due care to inspect, detect, and correct the gate that held 40 potentially dangerous animals.

**Special Duty**

Special duty of care may arise when a landowner-occupier is involved.

Here, David as an occupier of land, next door to his neighbor Peter, may owe a special duty of due care not to cause unreasonable risk of harm.

Peter was his next-door neighbor and his land abutted his and was at risk for unreasonable risk of harm if David failed to inspect, detect and correct any malfunction on his land that may ultimately cause damage to his neighbor's property or person.

David may have failed as an owner or occupier of land in his duty of due care to outsiders, in close proximity to his land, that may get injured.

**Breach of Duty**

Breach of duty arises when the person fails to exercise due care under the circumstances as a reasonably prudent person under the same or similar circumstances.

Here, the damage is clear and the facts show Peter was injured by David's failure to act as a reasonable rancher in securing his animals safely.

One of the locks on a gate into a pen that held 40 of his animals was beginning to pull free from the wooden support post to which the lock was attached. Notably, a close inspection would have revealed that the wood was rotting around the screws that attached the lock the 10-year-old post. Unfortunately, David failed to examine the gate support post when he performed his regular semi-annual inspection of the fencing on his land.

A reasonable owner or possessor of a herd of animals would have secured it properly and David failed to do so. The risk of harm far outweighed the utility of not fixing the gate, in light of the facts of this case, where Peter suffered a grave injury.

**Causation**

**Actual**

But for David's negligence in not securing the gate holding 40 potentially dangerous animals, Peter would not have been gored and butted and injured.

In addition, there was a subsequent act, namely the negligence of the emergency room not to stabilize Peter for concussion, that acted upon the injury actually caused by David.

**Proximate**

Proximate cause refers to the legal liability of David as to whether he is directly liable for Peter's injuries, without any supervening acts.

Here, David was the proximate cause of David's injuries as he was the direct cause of his injuries, and responsible for any foreseeable damage, and injury.

However, the emergency room team failed to check and stabilize Peter for his concussion, resulting in cerebral hemorrhage and paralysis in his upper limbs. This failure was an intervening act that acted upon Peter's injuries.

Notably, rescue or emergency acts aggravating a pre-existing injury are foreseeable and dependent causes, and do not cut David's legal responsibility in Peter's injuries.

Thus, both David and the Emergency room are the proximate cause of Peter's injuries.

## Damages

Damages are those that are foreseeable results of a negligent injury of another.

Here, as a result of David's negligence, Peter suffered a serious concussion, broken bones, and ultimately cerebral hemorrhage. The injuries were exacerbated by the negligence of the Emergency room staff.

## Joint Tortfeasors

When two or more actors jointly cause an indivisible injury they are both jointly and severally liable for the injury.

Here, The ER and David together are jointly and severally liable for Peter's injury, one indivisible injury.

Peter or his estate can sue both David and/or ER for his injury.

## Contribution

David can seek contribution from ER for their share.

**What defenses if any can David reasonably raise? Discuss.**

## Comparative Negligence

Under comparative theory, the damages are assigned according to the blameworthiness of each tortfeasor and share is allocated accordingly.

Here, David may assert Peter's comparative negligence as a defense.

He is unlikely to succeed as Peter may have acted reasonably under the circumstances.

**Assumption of Risk**

When one party knowingly, consciously and willfully confronts a risk, he will be deemed to have assumed the risk.

Here, David may argue that Peter knew and understood that these animals were dangerous and proceeded to herd them and in fact used an electric cattle prod and agitated the animals and causing them to attack.

David may not succeed in this defense if Peter acted reasonably under the circumstances.

**Contributory Negligence**

If a Plaintiff falls short in his own protection by failing to act as a reasonable and prudent man he may be contributorily negligent.

Here, David will argue that Peter used an electric cattle prod and exercised less than due care in his defense and contributed to his own injuries.

David is unlikely to use this defense if Peter acted reasonably under the circumstances.

In addition, David may not use this defense for his strict liability under strict liability case as discussed above.

**What damages, if any, will Peter be able to obtain against David?**

**Remedies**

## Monetary

Monetary damages are those that flow from the injury and are relatively certain and not remote and ascertainable.

## General

General damages refer to pain and suffering (past, present and future) that Peter will endure and are compensable.

## Special

Special damages are pecuniary damages in the form of medical bills, lost wages, profits, that Peter will suffer. He will be compensated for his medical bills and future bills, reduced to present value.

## Equitable

### Injunction

Peter or his estate may seek injunction against David to stop the milk farm to continue as it presents a dangerous activity.

# QUESTION 4

Jack, a retiree, plans to build a new home on his vacant property. He decided to use a particular product called "Austin Brown Stone" for the exterior walls, and estimated he would need about 100 tons of stone.

Jack drafted a contract to present to Stone-Co, a local stone distributor, in which Jack agreed: (i) to buy all the Austin Brown Stone he needs to build the exterior walls of his house, (ii) at a price of $200 per ton, (iii) to be delivered to his property in 5-ton lots within 10 days following each request for 5 tons, (iv) to be paid for upon delivery. To ensure timely deliveries, Jack included a liquidated damages clause which provided that Stone-Co would pay $5,000 per day for each day that any requested delivery is late.

Jack signed and dropped off the contract to Stone-Co for its review and signature. That evening, the Stone-Co salesperson, knowing that Austin Brown Stone is often not easily obtained, wrote the following just below Jack's liquidated damages clause: "Notwithstanding the foregoing, if Stone-Co has difficulty getting Austin Brown Stone, Stone-Co may substitute Austin White Stone."

The Stone-Co salesperson then signed the contract and returned it to Jack the next day. Jack did not read the modified contract or see the term added by Stone-Co.

One week later, Jack made a request for the first 5 tons of Austin Brown Stone, and Stone-Co started looking for a supplier. Stone-Co quickly discovered that Austin Brown Stone was not available in the United States. Although it could be imported from Canada, importing it would add $25 per ton to Stone-Co's expenses and reduce its profit margin.

Ten days after Jack's order, Stone-Co delivered Austin White Stone with a note stating that Austin Brown Stone was not available in the U.S., and a demand for payment at the new price of $225 per ton. Jack immediately called the Stone-Co salesperson, stating he would not accept the substitution because Austin White Stone is a completely different product.

Jack contracted with another supplier for Austin Brown Stone at $225 per ton. Jack thereafter filed a lawsuit against Stone-Co seeking damages for breach of contract and liquidated damages.

1. What is Jack's likelihood of success in his lawsuit and what damages, if any, would he be entitled to? Discuss.

2. What defenses, if any, can Stone-Co reasonably assert? Discuss.

# QUESTION 4: SELECTED ANSWER A

## 1. Jack v. Stone-Co

### Applicable law

For <u>sale of goods,</u> the applicable law is the <u>Uniform Commercial Code</u> (UCC), as opposed to other contracts, which are subject to the common law.

Here, the contract is for supply of stones, so this is sale of goods and the applicable law is therefore the UCC.

### Contract?

To have a valid contract, the following elements must be met:

- <u>willingness to be bound</u> by a legally enforceable contract by both parties,
- <u>mutual assent</u> (usually in the form of <u>offer</u> and <u>acceptance</u>),
- <u>consideration.</u>

Here, both parties (Jack and Stone-Co) intended to enter into a binding contract, so the willingness to be bound element is satisfied.

### Offer

An offer is an <u>expression of willingness to contract under certain terms,</u> made with the <u>intention that it shall become binding as soon as it is accepted by</u> the person to whom it Is addressed.

Here, the contract Jack left at the Stone-Co office contained all material terms of his offer, including price, quantity and time for delivery.

This was obviously an offer capable of acceptance by Stone-Co.

**Acceptance**

At common law, acceptance is a <u>final and unqualified expression of assent</u> to the terms of an offer.

Under the <u>UCC</u>, the mirror image rule, by which the expression of assent must be unqualified, has been modified and the <u>terms agreed to depend on the status of the parties</u> (i.e. whether both parties are <u>merchants</u> or not).

Where at <u>least one party is not a merchant</u>, if acceptance varies or adds a term to the offer, <u>acceptance is nonetheless still valid</u> and the <u>added or varied term</u> is considered as a <u>mere offer to vary or add the term.</u>

Here, Jack was not acting as a merchant (he is not in the trade of stones and, even though he apparently knows pretty well how to draft contracts, he did not claim himself to be a merchant or particularly knowledgeable about the trade of stones).

Therefore, the terms of the contract were those of the original offer he made, unless he expressly agreed to the added term Stone-Co's salesman had put in the contract, and the acceptance is still valid (under UCC rules), because Stone-Co did not explicitly limit its acceptance by requesting that Jack accepts himself the additional term about the Austin White Stone.

So, the mutual assent element is satisfied, with the terms of the original offer (made by Jack) as the terms of the contract (and Stone-Co's additional term being a mere proposal to add the term to the contract and which, under these circumstances, has not been accepted by Jack and is not part of the contract).

**Consideration**

Consideration is satisfied where the contract is the result of a <u>bargained-for agreement</u> and each party suffered <u>legal benefit or detriment.</u>

Usually, <u>quantity is required</u> for a valid consideration to be found in a contract but <u>requirements and output contracts</u> are considered valid and <u>satisfy the consideration requirement.</u>

Here, the contract is a requirements contract (all stone that Jack will need for building his house) and, even though it states no particular quantity, there is valid consideration (Jack to pay the price, Stone-Co to provide the stones).

Therefore, consideration is satisfied for this contract and there is a valid, enforceable contract between Jack and Stone-Co.

**Liquidated damages clause**

To be valid, a liquidated damages clause must reflect the <u>damages, which would have been reasonably anticipated by the parties at the time they entered into the contract.</u> An unreasonable amount would be deemed a <u>penalty clause</u> and would <u>not be enforceable</u> by the court.

Here, the liquidated damages clause mentions that Stone-Co will be liable to Jack for $5,000 for each day of delay in delivering the stones for each order delayed. This represents a substantial amount compared to the price of the contract: each delivery must be of 5 tons, at $200 per ton, i.e., each delivery is $1,000. The liquidated damages clause therefore represents 5 times the price of the goods to be delivered for each day of delay!

And Jack's estimation of needs is 100 tons of stone, i.e., about $20,000 for the whole contract.

A four day delay would result in Stone-Co's liability for the estimated price of the whole contract, which is apparently totally unreasonable.

The only justification would be if the delay in delivering the stones could result in Jack having a substantial loss of earning, revenue or another form of liability himself. As he is building his own house, he would not be liable to a client or another contractor for the delay in performing the job.

However, he might have other contractors charge him for the day without stone, but $5,000 is unlikely to be a reasonable amount on these facts (unless wages are huge in Jack's area...) and the clause would be considered a penalty clause, therefore not enforceable by the court.

**Damages**

On these facts, the liquidated damages clause would be considered as a penalty clause and would not be enforceable by the court, so Jack could not recover the $5,000 per day for each day of late delivery.

However, he could recover the damages suffered by the breach of contract by Stone-Co, i.e., the additional $25 he would have to pay for each ton of stones required for building his house.

## 2. Stone-Co's defenses

### Impracticability

Where performance of a contract becomes impossible because of <u>circumstances not caused by either party</u> (but outside their control), performance is excused.

Under modern common law, if performance becomes <u>substantially more difficult,</u> so as to <u>affect the nature of performance</u>, the same rule can apply (impracticability instead of impossibility).

Here, Stone-Co could try to rely on the defense of impracticability to explain that they were unable to provide Austin Brown Stone to Jack, because this type of stone was not available on the US market.

However, this is unlikely to be a valid defense on the facts, as Jack obtained the Austin Brown Stone from another supplier, and it seems not to have been so difficult or impossible to obtain the stones in question in the US. It must have been merely more expensive, and a bad bargain is never an excuse for breach of contract, so Stone-Co is unlikely to prevail with this defense.

### Lack of consideration

*C.f. supra for definition of consideration.*

Here, as stated above, requirements contracts are valid contracts, so Stone-Co could not rely on the lack of consideration to try to avoid liability under this contract.

# QUESTION 4:  SELECTED ANSWER B

## Applicable Law

The UCC applies to the sale of goods; tangible, movable items at the time of sale.  The common law applies to all other transactions.

Here, we are dealing with the purchase of stone, to build a wall.  The stone is tangible and movable; therefore it is a good.

The UCC laws will apply.

## Merchants

A merchant under the UCC is someone who holds himself out to have special knowledge or skill particular to the goods of the sale, or regular deals with the goods of the kind.

Here, Jack is a retiree and plans on building a new home on his vacant property.  There are no facts to show that Jack has any special knowledge or skill related to the Austin Brown Stone, or that he regularly deals with the home.  It is likely he is purchasing the stone for this one period in time, to build himself a home.

Stone-Co, is a local stone distributor, they sell stones, and regularly deals with stones in their business.

Jack will not be considered a merchant under the UCC, but Stone-Co is a merchant.

## Valid Contract

A valid contract consists of mutual assent through offer and acceptance, consideration, and no defenses to formation.

## Offer

An offer is an objective manifestation of intent to be bound, given with specific and definite terms, to an identified offeree.

Here, Jack has drafted a contract to present to Stone-Co, which contained the following terms:

subject matter: Austin Brown Stone
price: $200 per ton, paid for upon delivery
delivery: delivered to his home in 5 ton lots within 10 days following each request for 5 tons.
quantity: all the stone needed to build the exterior walls of his home.

His offer is certain and definite in its terms, and a reasonable person would think that Jack intended to enter into a contract and create the power of acceptance in Stone-Co. Furthermore, he signed and dropped off the contract to Stone-Co, so he communicated his intent to enter into a contract.

Jack has made a valid offer.

## Requirements Contract

Under the UCC, a party can agree to purchase all goods required for their needs, and the other party may agree to supply all of the goods required. This is called a requirements contract.

Typically, a contract for goods must include quantity; however, in a requirements contract, all that is needed is the good faith promise that the purchaser will purchase all that is required for their needs. This contract will not be found to be illusory and lack of definiteness because both parties are to act in good faith.

Jack will be bound by the requirements contract to act in good faith.

## Acceptance

An acceptance is an objective manifestation of unequivocal assent to the terms of the offer, communicated in a proper manner and time. Under common law, acceptance must be the "mirror image" of the terms of the offer; however, under the UCC, acceptance can be given in any reasonable manner.

The next day, Stone-Co's salesperson signed the contract and returned it to Jack the next day after adding a term. Since her contract had an additional term, it would have been a counteroffer under common law but the UCC allows for acceptance in any reasonable manner. Since the contract was not worded so that acceptance was conditional on the additional term but rather, it stated that "notwithstanding the foregoing", it is still a valid acceptance.

Therefore, Stone-Co has accepted Jack's offer.

## Consideration

Consideration is a bargained-for exchange, whereby both parties incur a new legal detriment.

Here, Jack's promise to pay for all required stones induced Stone-Co's promise to deliver all required stones. Both parties have incurred new legal detriment.

Valid consideration exists.

## Additional Terms under UCC

Between merchants, additional terms will be automatically added to the contract unless the contract limits it, the term materially alters the contract, or the other party rejects within 10 days. Between a merchant and a non-merchant, additional terms will be considered proposals to the contract and will not automatically be added to the contract.

Here, Jack did not read the modified contract, or see the term added by Stone-Co. Therefore, the proposal of the additional terms have not been added to the contract since Jack did not assent to the terms.

Jack and Stone-Co have a requirements contract for Austin Brown Stone.

## Modification

A modification under common law required mutual assent and consideration. A modification to a UCC contract does not require consideration, only mutual assent and good faith.

10 days after Jack's order, Stone-Co attempts to modify the contract because Austin Brown Stone is not available in the United States and importing it would incur additional costs. Stone-Co's request for modification was in good faith; however, Jack did not assent to the terms because Austin White Stone is a completely different stone.

There has not been a valid modification.

## Breach

Breach is the failure to perform one's duties under contract.

All contracts can be substantially performed, unless there is a term that is expressly stated in the contract. Furthermore, sale of goods under the UCC require "Perfect Tender", and must be exactly as ordered.

Here, the contract between Jack and Stone-Co expressly states that the 5-ton lots must be delivered to his home within 10 days following each request for 5 tons. Jack made his first request for stones one week after contracting. 10 days later, Stone-Co failed to deliver the required stones, but rather notified Jack that the stones weren't available in the United States and that he would have to pay additional fees if he wanted them imported from Canada.

Furthermore, instead of sending Austin Brown Stone, they delivered Austin White Stone. As discussed above, Stone-Co's request to allow substitution for Austin White Stone was not added into the contract; therefore Stone-Co breached by sending nonconforming goods.

Stone-Co has not perfectly tendered the goods required by Jack and failed to deliver Austin Brown Stone within 10 days of Jack's request.

Stone-Co has breached the contract.

## Anticipatory Breach

Where a party has unequivocally expressed his inability to perform under contract, the other party may sue immediately, or wait for performance to be due, then sue.

Here, on the 10th day after requesting delivery, Stone-Co has sent non-conforming stones and called Jack and expressed the difficulties in getting Austin Brown Stone, and requested a higher payment to get it to him. They have unequivocally expressed their inability and unwillingness to perform their duties under contract for further deliveries of the required stones, which is to deliver Austin Brown Stone at $200 per ton.

Stone-Co has anticipatorily breached the rest of the contract, and Jack may sue immediately.

## Damages

Liquidated Damages

Liquidated damages are valid when damages are unforeseeable at the time of contracting, are reasonable in amount, and not a penalty.

Here, Jack would likely incur damages for the late delivery of stone because he would lose time; however liquidated damages amount at $5000/day is likely to be deemed a punishment. It is unreasonable in amount, and furthermore, the damages that Jack would incur are likely to be foreseeable.

Jack will not be able to recover the liquidated damages, and will have to look to Expectation Damages.

## Expectation Damages

The non-breaching party is entitled to what their expected benefits are under contract.

Here, Stone-Co has breached the contract and Jack will be entitled to expectation damages. Jack expected to purchase about 100 tons of stone at $200 per ton, which comes out to roughly $20,000. He ended up contracting with another supplier for $225 per ton, an extra $25 per ton, which is roughly an additional $2,500 more than he expected to pay. Jack will be entitled to recover from Stone-Co $25 for every ton he needed to build his wall.

Furthermore, he will be entitled to any incidental costs related to the breach, and any reliance damages which were incurred as a result of his reliance on the contract.

2. What defenses, if any, can Stone-Co reasonably assert?

## Impossibility

A contract is deemed impossible when unforeseen at the time of contracting and objectively speaking, no other person could possibly perform the contract.

Here, Stone-Co will assert that the contract was Impossible to satisfy because the stone was not available in the United States. However, since Stone-Co is able to import the stone from Canada at an additional cost, and Jack found another supplier who was able to supply him with the stone, the contract will not be Impossible.

## Impracticability

A contract because impracticable when unforeseen at the time of contracting, the contract becomes impracticable to perform.

Here, Stone-Co will claim impracticability because of the added costs of importing the goods from Canada, which would cut into their profit margin. Increased costs will be deemed to make a contract impracticable, only if it is a substantial increase to the cost. Here, the extra costs of importing the rock adds $25 per ton of rock. It is not substantially increased and rather small, especially because it seems that it would not take away Stone-Co's entire profit, but rather merely reduce the profit margin. To void a contract due to increased costs, the cost would have to be at least 10 times the expected cost, and cause substantial hardship to Stone-Co. We do not have this situation here.

Furthermore, the stones were not available at the time of contracting, and had Stone-Co done their due diligence, they would have figured that out; but instead, they agreed to the contract without checking, then failed to perform.

The contract will not be deemed impracticable.

Stone-Co has no valid defenses.